Sous Vide

Modern Techniques for Perfect Cooking Through Science (Scrumptious Dinners, Gourmet Cookbook, Precision Cooking)

Sarah P. Williamson

Sous Vide: Modern Techniques for Perfect Cooking Through Science (Scrumptious Dinners, Gourmet Cookbook, Precision Cooking)

Table of Contents

1 - Introduction

Benefits of Cooking the Sous Vide Way

Sous vide sounds too fancy to apply to cooking, but it simply means placing your ingredients in a container (a cooking pouch or canning jar can be used) and then dropping the container into a heated water bath set at a target temperature. As soon as your food reaches the intended time or temperature, you remove it from the water bath, finish (for example, by giving it a quick sear) it, and enjoy it.

Everything Tastes Better

Cooking the sous vide way gives you food that simply tastes way better than if you cooked it using conventional methods. Your tenderloin steaks turn out juicier and perfectly done around the edges, your beef or lamb ribs almost melt as they touch your mouth, your fish fillets are succulent and their centers are as evenly cooked as their edges.

Even an egg can be cooked the sous vide way, and you will be amazed at how delicate and custard-like your poached egg turns out.

Carved in History

Since the ancient times, the practice of preserving and cooking different kinds of food in sealed containers or packages has been around. Culinary history records will tell you that people have been wrapping food in leaves, sealing them inside the bladders of animals, packing them in salt, or potting them in fat prior to cooking.

They already had the idea that preventing food from being exposed to air can slow down its decay - something that vacuum sealing successfully does. As a bonus, packaging your food also helps keep it succulent, not dried out.

Precision, Perfection

"Sous vide" is a French term that means "under vacuum." The sous vide cooking method does utilize vacuum sealing food, but its important feature is precise temperature control. Cooking your food the sous vide way means you use a heater that is computer-controlled to bring a water bath to the target temperature and then keep the water bath at that temperature for hours or days.

Having the ability to control temperature or heat in cooking your food gives you the freedom to go about the cooking process without being a slave to time.

When using the conventional oven or grill, you have to deal with extreme temperatures as well as fluctuating temperatures – this is why it is important to get your exact cooking times straight, since going a little off the mark results in foods that do not turn out as they should.

But if you cook using the sous vide method, your foods are guaranteed to taste just right, giving you ample time to focus on the other aspects of food preparation.

But First, Safety

The sous vide way of cooking's use of accurate and uniform temperatures provide you other benefits:

Your food turn out evenly cooked through, so you can say goodbye to rare centers and overly dried-out edges; you get the same perfectly cooked results every single time you cook; and most importantly, you can rest assured that any potential pathogens in your food, especially in chicken and other poultry meats, are killed for your safety.

Have It All

Lastly, cooking your food in a closed container allows you to provide a completely humid environment for your ingredients. This is what braises your food in an effective manner and gives you markedly more scrumptious and more succulent results.

Simply searing your sous vide cooked food (which do not brown) will give them those traditional flavors you have gotten used to, so you actually get to enjoy both the nostalgic taste of your old style cooking and the gourmet flavors imparted by the scientific sous vide method.

Tips and Tricks for Sous Vide Cooking

Digging into gourmet quality dishes does not have to be tricky. Simplify sous vide cooking by following these tips:

Pouching

Prepping your food for sous vide cooking is as easy as buy, portion, and seal:

1. Purchase economy size packages of chicken, fish, and steak.

2. Divide your meats and other proteins into individual servings, then place each serving into individual cooking pouches.

3. Don't forget to include your favorite seasonings before vacuum sealing the cooking pouch.

2 - Saving Time on Cooking

Cutting down on your cooking time has never been easier:

Cook, then freeze

- Season your food and place in the cooking pouches.
- Vacuum seal and place in the sous vide water oven to cook.
- Place the cooking pouches in an ice bath for thirty to forty-five minutes.
- Label the pouches with date and contents.
- Place in the freezer (use within a year).
- Take the pouch out of the freezer and thaw.
- Reheat for forty-five minutes for every inch of thickness.
- When reheating from frozen, reheat for thirty minutes more.
- Sear the reheated food and serve immediately with or without sauce.

Freeze, then cook

- Season your individual servings of fish, seafood, poultry, meat, or game.
- Place in the cooking pouches and vacuum seal.
- Write the date and contents on the label.
- Freeze the pouches with uncooked ingredients for no more than six weeks.
- Remove the pouches from the freezer and allow to thaw.
- Place in the sous vide water oven to cook at the target temperature.
- If cooking from frozen, cook for an additional thirty minutes.
- Serve sauced or seared.

Marinating

Marinate your foods with sous vide ease:

1. Place your fish/ meat/ poultry, vegetables, and other

ingredients in the cooking pouch. Add the marinade and then press with your hands (to remove air pockets) before sealing manually.

2. Place the cooking pouch in the freezer to allow the marinade to set.
3. Take the pouch out of the freezer and cut through the pouch (below the seal).
4. Vacuum seal the pouch and submerge in the sous vide water oven (preheated to target temperature). If cooking from frozen, allow to cook for an additional thirty minutes.

3 - Cooking Efficiently

Group similar food to save time:

Cooking vegetables

You can cook most vegetables in the temperature range of 183 degrees Fahrenheit to 185 degrees Fahrenheit. The food will generally become tender within forty-five minutes to one hour in the sous vide water oven.

To save time, you can submerge several cooking pouches containing different types of vegetables in the sous vide water oven all at once. You can then consume the cooked vegetables for several days. This trick may have you spending some hands-on veggie prepping time.

It does allow you to literally just leave them to cook on their own. While your sous vide water oven is cooking all the vegetables you need for the next three days, you can work on your exercise routine, play with your baby, or watch your favorite TV reruns.

Cooking meats

You can cook meats (beef, duck, lamb, ostrich, bison, and other red meats – placed inside different cooking pouches) at the same time and at the same sous vide water oven temperature of 134 degrees Fahrenheit (for that perfectly medium-rare doneness). Just keep in mind that the length of cooking time will vary, depending on the toughness as well as the thickness of the meat cut.

If you would rather have your meat cooked medium or well-done, simply set your sous vide water oven to 140 degrees or 150 degrees Fahrenheit. Any which way, you can rest assured that your meat will be cooked evenly from the center to the edges.

After seasoning your meats, portion them according to your needs and then place inside their cooking pouches. Vacuum seal before cooking all at once in the sous vide water oven at their target temperature.

Once cooked, remove the pouches from the sous vide water oven and place in an ice bath. Dry off the pouches before labeling with their respective dates and contents, then place in the refrigerator to chill for up to two days, or place in the freezer to keep for up to one year.

Cooking tougher meat cuts

Tougher meat cuts include spare ribs, roasts, and grass-fed

beef. Simply tenderize overnight by cooking for 8 to 10 hours or more.

Cooking poultry

You can cook chicken meat (or turkey) along with pork at the temperature range of 140 degrees Fahrenheit to 146 degrees Fahrenheit for two hours to two hours and thirty minutes. Submerge up to 12 chicken breasts, or 8 turkey breasts, or 6 pork tenderloins, or 16 pork chops, or any combination of these meats.

As soon as they are cooked, remove from the sous vide water oven and their cooking pouches, then submerge in an ice bath. Dry off and label before refrigerating for up to two days or freezing up to one year.

Reheating previously cooked food

While your fish is cooking in the sous vide water oven, you can add in pouches containing cooked veggies to reheat them. A ½-inch fish fillet's delicate flesh only requires 20 to 40 minutes of cooking, so you can drop and reheat one to two pouches of cooked veggies in the sous vide water oven as the fish cooks.

Doing it this way allows you to have delicious, nutritious, and effortless dinner ready within just 30 to 40 minutes.

Multitask cooking

As long as there is enough space in the sous vide water oven, you can cook pork spare ribs for thirty hours at 176 degrees along with chicken, turkey, or duck leg quarters (which also cook at the same target temperature).

4 - Succulent Sous Vide Fish for Dinner Recipes

Dill Caper and Artichoke Salmon

Ingredients:

Salmon:

- Kosher salt (1/2 cup)
- Dill, fresh, chopped (1 teaspoon)
- Liquid smoke, Applewood (1 tablespoon)
- Salmon steaks, boned removed, 2" (4 pieces)
- Brown sugar (1/2 cup)
- Pepper, freshly ground (1/2 teaspoon)
- Olive oil, extra virgin (2 tablespoons)

Artichokes:

- Lemon juice, freshly squeezed (1/2 tablespoon)
- Artichokes, trimmed, w/choke removed (4 pieces)
- Salt (1/4 teaspoon)

- Pepper, freshly ground (1/4 teaspoon)

Sauce:

- Butter, melted (4 ounces)
- Dill, fresh, chopped (1 tablespoon)
- Dijon mustard (1/2 teaspoon)
- Egg yolks (3 pieces)
- Capers, chopped (1 tablespoon)
- Salt (1/2 teaspoon + ¼ teaspoon)
- Lemon juice, freshly squeezed (1 tablespoon + ½ tablespoon)

Directions:

1. Place the pepper, sugar, and dill in a medium bowl. Add the salt and liquid smoke. Stir to combine into a paste. Rub all surfaces of the salmon steaks with the paste, making sure they are evenly covered. Place the salmon steaks on a large plate, then wrap with cling film before placing in the refrigerator for one hour.

2. Rinse the steaks thoroughly until all traces of the paste are gone. Use paper towels to pat dry afterwards. Working in batches, place the steaks inside cooking pouches. Vacuum seal the pouches before placing in the refrigerator until cooking time.

3. Fill the sous vide water oven and then preheat to 185 degrees.

4. Meanwhile, trim and peel the artichoke stems before rubbing with lemon juice. Place in a cooking pouch, vacuum seal, and submerge in the sous vide water oven. Cook for about one hour and fifteen minutes or until tenderly cooked. Transfer the pouch containing the artichokes onto a plate before lowering the sous vide water oven's temperature to 149 degrees.

5. Fill a cooking pouch with the ingredients for the sauce. Vacuum seal before submerging in the sous vide water oven to cook for forty-five minutes. Once done, transfer to a blender filled with capers and dill. Process until well-emulsified and thick, pour into a cooking pouch, and vacuum seal. Place in the sous vide water oven again to keep warm (do the same to

the cooked artichokes).

6. Lower the sous vide water oven temperature further to 134 degrees. Drop the pouch containing the chilled salmon steaks and allow to cook for one hour along with the artichokes and sauce.
7. In the meantime, heat a well-greased grill until extremely hot.
8. Once the salmon steaks are done. Then remove from the water oven and set on a tray. Do the same with the artichokes.
9. Brush a bit of olive oil on all sides of the salmon steaks and artichokes, then sprinkle pepper and salt on the artichokes alone. Place the salmon steaks on the grill and cook for thirty seconds on each side or until seared and golden; repeat with the artichokes. Once done, transfer onto a serving platter (warmed), making sure the artichokes surround the salmon.
10. Take the sauce out of the sous vide water oven and pour on top of the salmon steaks and artichokes. Serve right away.

Easy and Delicious Salmon

Ingredients:

- Kosher salt (1 ½ teaspoons)
- Butter, unsalted, sliced into 4 portions (28 grams)
- King salmon, skinless, boneless, 6 ounces (4 pieces)
- Lemon slices, fresh (4 pieces)

Directions:

1. Fill the sous vide water oven before preheating to 126 degrees.
2. Meanwhile, sprinkle salt on the salmon pieces before topping each with a slice of lemon and a portion of butter.
3. Transfer 2 salmon portions into a cooking pouch. Vacuum seal the two pouches before submerging in the sous vide water oven. Cook for twenty minutes.
4. Meanwhile, heat a skillet before adding a little oil.
5. Once the salmon is done, remove from the sous vide

water and transfer onto the hot, greased skillet. Cook for one to two minutes or until the salmon pieces are caramelized on the surface.

6. Serve and enjoy.

Yummy Cranberry Salmon

Ingredients:

- Cilantro, fresh, chopped (a handful)
- Salmon fillets, boneless, skinless, 5 ounces (2 pieces)
- Marinade:
- Barbecue sauce (2 tablespoons)
- Cranberry juice (1 tablespoon)
- Salt (1/8 teaspoon)
- Cranberry sauce (2 tablespoons)
- Olive oil, extra virgin (1 tablespoon)
- Lime juice, freshly squeezed (1 teaspoon)

Directions:

4 - SUCCULENT SOUS VIDE FISH FOR DINNER RECIPES

1. Place all the ingredients for the marinade in a medium bowl. Stir to combine. Set aside 1½ tablespoons of the mixture for using later in a separate step.

2. Place the salmon fillets in the marinade and coat with the mixture on all sides. Cover the bowl before placing in the refrigerator for one to two hours.

3. Meanwhile, fill the sous vide water oven before preheating to 140 degrees.

4. Take the marinated salmon fillets out of the refrigerator and transfer into a cooking pouch. Vacuum seal, place in the sous vide water oven and cook for twenty-five to thirty minutes.

5. Set the broiler on high to preheat.

6. Once the salmon fillets are done. Then transfer to a pan (broiler-safe). Coat with the marinade you set aside earlier before placing in the broiler. Cook for one to two minutes or until heated through.

7. Top with chopped cilantro and serve immediately. Enjoy.

Chili Maple and Lemon Salmon

Ingredients:

- Sea salt, spiced (1 ½ tablespoons)
- Parsley, curly, freshly chopped (4 tablespoons)
- Maple syrup (4 ounces)
- Leeks, chopped (1 2/3 cups)
- Lemon zest, finely grated (1 tablespoon)
- Salmon fillet, fresh, scaled, 2 ½-oz. (4 pieces)
- Castor sugar (1 ½ tablespoons)
- Double cream (3 tablespoons + 1 teaspoon)
- Red chili, small (1 piece)
- Lemons, halved, caramelized (2 pieces)

Directions:

1. Mix the sugar and salt together before sprinkling on the fish fillets. Place the seasoned fillets in a large bowl, cover, and refrigerate for two hours.

2. Meanwhile, fill the sous vide water oven before preheating to 115 degrees.

3. Take the chilled fish fillets out of the refrigerator and lightly rinse before patting dry with paper towels and placing inside cooking pouches. After vacuum sealing the pouches, submerge in the preheated sous vide water oven. Allow the fish fillets to cook for forty-five minutes.

4. In the meantime, heat a water-filled pan on high. Allow the water to boil before adding the chopped leeks and salt. Boil for another two to three minutes, then drain and rinse with cold water. Drain again before squeezing the leeks until thoroughly dry. Place in a small bowl and set aside.

5. Heat another pan on medium. Add the cream and allow to boil to slightly thicken it. Stir in the leeks and cook for one to two minutes or until warmed through. Stir in the black pepper and salt. Then reduce heat to low to keep the mixture warm.

6. Heat another saucepan (small) on medium after pouring in the maple syrup. Once the syrup is cara-

melized, cover the pan and set aside to keep warm.

7. Slice the chili into lengthwise halves before removing the stems and deseeding. Mince the flesh and stir into the maple syrup. Stir in the lemon zest, black pepper, and chopped parsley as well.
8. After taking the cooked salmon out of the sous vide water bath, pat dry with paper towels and brush with the maple syrup mixture.
9. Meanwhile, pour the leek mixture onto a platter. Add the salmon on top.
10. Serve drizzled with more maple syrup mixture and enjoy.

Italian Style Poached Cod

Ingredients:

Cod:

- Olive oil, extra virgin (3 tablespoons)
- Lemon zest (1/2 tablespoon)

4 - SUCCULENT SOUS VIDE FISH FOR DINNER RECIPES

- Cod fillets, skinless, 6-oz. (2 pieces)
- Parsley sprigs, fresh (2 pieces)
- Peppers & olives:
- Red peppers, roasted, chopped (1/3 cup)
- Black olives, sliced (1/3 cup)
- Salt, kosher (1/4 teaspoon)
- Pepper, freshly cracked (1/4 teaspoon)
- Onion, small, peeled, diced (1 piece)
- Rosemary, fresh, chopped finely (1 teaspoon)
- Red pepper flakes (a pinch)

Salsa:

- Garlic clove, peeled, crushed (1 piece)
- Balsamic vinegar (1 teaspoon)
- Salt, kosher (1/4 teaspoon)
- Pepper, freshly cracked (1/4 teaspoon)

- Plum tomatoes, sliced (1 ¼ cups)
- Olive oil, extra virgin (1 teaspoon)
- Paprika, smoked (1/4 teaspoon)

Directions:

1. Fill the sous vide water oven before preheating to 181 degrees.
2. Fill a cooking pouch (small) with the tomatoes. Add the olive oil and garlic, then vacuum seal and place in the sous vide water oven. Cook for forty-five minutes before transferring into the blender. Add the smoked paprika and vinegar, then process until well-blended and smooth. Season with pepper and salt before setting aside.
3. Lower the sous vide water oven's temperature to 132 degrees.
4. Heat a skillet on medium-high before adding olive oil. Stir in the diced onions and cook for three minutes or until translucent and fragrant. Add the red pepper, olives, and rosemary; stir to combine

with the onions. Reduce heat to medium and cook for an additional four to six minutes before sprinkling salt and pepper into the mixture. Remove from heat and set aside.

5. Place the fish inside a cooking pouch (large). Add the salt, pepper, and olive oil before vacuum sealing the pouch. Submerge into the sous vide water oven to cook for twenty minutes.
6. Meanwhile, pour the tomato mixture onto a plate. Once the fish is cooked, place on top of the tomato mixture. Pour the onions and olives over the fish before garnishing with fresh parsley.
7. Serve sprinkled with lemon zest.

5 - Evenly Tender Sous Vide Poultry for Dinner Recipes

Paleo Friendly Crispy Chicken

Ingredients:

- Butter, unsalted (6 tablespoons)
- Black pepper, freshly ground (1/2 teaspoon)
- Garlic powder (1/4 teaspoon)
- Thyme, dried (1/4 teaspoon)
- Kosher salt (1/4 teaspoon)
- Lard (2 tablespoons)
- Chicken thighs, boneless, skin-on (6 pieces)

Directions:

1. Fill the sous vide water oven before preheating to 150 degrees.
2. Pat the chicken thighs with paper towels to dry after flattening them. Season with pepper, salt, dried thyme, and garlic powder on the skinless side.

3. Rub butter (1 tablespoon) on each chicken thigh before placing inside the cooking pouch. Vacuum seal before submerging in the preheated sous vide water oven. Allow the chicken thighs to cook for one hour and thirty minutes.

4. Meanwhile, heat a skillet on medium before adding lard. Once the lard is smoking, add the cooked chicken thighs. With their skin sides down, cook for about three to five minutes or until the skins are crisp. Once done, allow the chicken thighs to drain on a wire rack after sprinkling the crisped skins with a little fleur de sel.

5. Place the chicken thighs alongside your favorite vegetables.

6. Serve and enjoy.

Extra Special Turkey

Ingredients:

- Water, filtered (2 quarts)
- Black peppercorns, whole (1 tablespoon)

5 - EVENLY TENDER SOUS VIDE POULTRY FOR DINNER RECIPES

- Butter (6 tablespoons)
- Turkey, whole, 10-pound (1 piece)
- Kosher salt (11 tablespoons)
- Poultry seasoning (1 tablespoon)
- Sage sprigs, fresh (3 pieces)

Directions:

1. Remove the breasts (with skin on) and leg quarters from the turkey and place in a large bowl; set aside. Reserve the carcass for making turkey stock later.
2. Meanwhile, fill a large pot with water. Add salt, poultry seasoning, and peppercorns; stir to combine.
3. Add the turkey pieces in the pot filled with herbed brine. Cover and place in the refrigerator to brine overnight.
4. Fill the sous vide water oven before preheating to 146 degrees.
5. Meanwhile, pat dry the turkey pieces with paper towels after rinsing well. Place each turkey piece in an in-

dividual cooking pouch. To each pouch, add 1 sage sprig and 2 tablespoons of butter before vacuum sealing.

6. Place the turkey leg quarters in the refrigerator while you cook the turkey breasts first. Submerge the breast pouches in the sous vide water oven; cook for four to six hours. Once done, transfer the breast pouches into an ice bath for a minimum of one hour (alternatively, you can place them in the refrigerator for no more than two days prior to finishing).

7. Raise the sous vide water oven's temperature to 176 degrees. Add the cooking pouches containing the leg quarters and cook for eight to twelve hours. Once done, transfer into an ice bath or refrigerate for one to two days prior to finishing.

8. Fill the sous vide water oven and then preheat to 146 degrees. Drop the breast pouches as well as leg quarter pouches for a minimum of one hour. Once the turkey pieces are reheated, remove from their pouches and pat dry using paper towels. Brush all sides with herbed butter (melted) and set aside.

9. Heat the broiler on high. Cook the turkey pieces for a few minutes or until the skins are seared and golden brown.

10. Serve and enjoy.

Arborio and Cremini Turkey

Ingredients:

- Olive oil, extra virgin (1 teaspoon)
- Garlic, minced, roasted (2 tablespoons)
- Salt, kosher (1/4 teaspoon)
- Pepper, freshly cracked (1/4 teaspoon)
- Cremini mushrooms, cleaned, sliced (10 pieces)
- Rosemary leaves, fresh, minced (1 tablespoon)
- Arborio rice (1 cup)
- Yellow onion, small, peeled, diced (1 piece)
- Turkey, cooked, diced (8 ounces)
- Turkey broth, reduced sodium (3 cups)

- Romano cheese, grated (1/3 cup)

Directions:

1. Fill the sous vide water oven before preheating to 183 degrees.
2. Heat a large skillet over medium. Then add the olive oil. Once heated through, stir in onions and mushrooms. Cook for four to five minutes or until tender and fragrant.
3. Transfer the sautéed onions and mushrooms into a cooking pouch (gallon size). Add all the other ingredients (save for the cheese) for this recipe before vacuum sealing the pouch.
4. Place the sealed pouch in the preheated sous vide water oven. Allow the mixture in the pouch to cook for forty-five minutes. Once done, transfer the pouch contents to a serving bowl (pre-warmed).
5. Use a fork to fluff the cooked rice before stirring in the cheese.
6. Serve right away.

Onion Chicken

Ingredients:

- Mustard oil (3 tablespoons + 1 teaspoon)
- Yogurt, natural, salted (4 ounces)
- Chicken breasts, boneless (2 pounds)
- Cilantro, fresh (a handful)
- Mint leaves, fresh (a handful)

Marinade:

- Ground coriander, powdered (1 tablespoon)
- Fenugreek, dry (1 teaspoon)
- Cilantro, fresh, chopped, divided (1 handful)
- Ginger garlic paste (2 tablespoons)
- Greek yogurt, low-fat, plain (3 tablespoons)
- Garam masala (2 tablespoons)
- Cayenne pepper, ground (1 teaspoon)

- Lemon juice, freshly squeezed (1 tablespoon)
- Food coloring, bright orange (1/4 teaspoon)
- Salt, kosher (1/4 teaspoon)

Onions:

- Fenugreek, dry (1 teaspoon)
- Red onions, large, peeled, sliced thinly (2 pieces)
- Balsamic vinegar (2 tablespoons)
- Olive oil, extra virgin (1 tablespoon)
- Salt, kosher (1/4 teaspoon)
- Brown sugar (1 tablespoon)

Directions:

1. Pat dry the chicken breasts after rinsing, then set aside.
2. Place the ingredients (set aside ½ of the fresh coriander for using later) for the marinade in a large bowl. Add the chicken breasts, turning to ensure all

sides are evenly coated with the marinade. Cover and place in the refrigerator to marinate for two hours.

3. Meanwhile, fill the sous vide water oven and preheat to 160 degrees.

4. Drain off all traces of marinade before placing the chicken breasts inside a cooking pouch. Vacuum seal and then place in the preheated sous vide water oven. Cook for two to three hours.

5. Meanwhile, heat a frying pan (nonstick) on medium-low. Add the olive oil and then stir in the onions. Add the salt and fenugreek, then sauté for about fifteen to twenty minutes or until onions are tender and caramelized. Stir in the balsamic vinegar as well as brown sugar, making sure the onions are well-coated. Once done, remove from heat and set aside.

6. Take the cooked chicken breasts out of the cooking pouch and drain. Pat dry with paper towels and place on a plate.

7. Heat a skillet (nonstick) on medium-high before adding the mustard oil. Once heated through, add the

chicken pieces and cook on each side for one to two minutes or until golden brown and nicely seared.

8. Transfer the chicken pieces onto a platter, alongside the caramelized onions. Top with fresh mint leaves and the reserved fresh coriander.
9. Serve and enjoy.

Easy Herbed Turkey with Cranberry Sauce

Ingredients:

- Salt, kosher (4 tablespoons)
- Butter, unsalted, divided (3 tablespoons)
- Black pepper, freshly ground (1/4 teaspoon)
- Olive oil, extra virgin (1 tablespoon)
- Water (2 cups)
- Black peppercorns (10 pieces)
- Sage leaves, fresh (4 pieces)

- Garlic cloves, roasted, minced finely (2 pieces)
- Cranberry sauce:
- Sugar, granulated (1 cup)
- Cranberries, fresh (12 ounces)
- Orange zest, freshly grated (1 tablespoon)

Directions:

1. Fill the sous vide water oven before preheating to 183 degrees.
2. Fill a cooking pouch with all the ingredients for the cranberry sauce. Vacuum seal before submerging in the preheated sous vide water oven to cook for one hour. Once the mixture is done, take the pouch out of the sous vide water oven and smash gently with your hands to make the cranberry sauce chunky. Quickly submerge the cranberry sauce pouch into an ice bath. After twenty minutes, place in the refrigerator for two to three days.
3. Fill a large cooking pouch (gallon size) with water and salt. Once the salt is dissolved, add the turkey

breast and peppercorns. Vacuum seal the pouch and place in the refrigerator for four hours to allow the turkey to brine.

4. Meanwhile, fill the sous vide water oven and preheat to 146 degrees.

5. Rinse the brined turkey before patting dry with paper towels. Sprinkle black pepper on all sides of the turkey and place inside a cooking pouch. Add butter (2 tablespoons), sage leaves, and garlic before vacuum sealing and submerging in the sous vide water oven. Allow the turkey to cook for three to four hours. Once done, pour the pouch juices into a small bowl and set aside for making gravy/sauce later. Pat dry the chicken pieces and set aside on a large plate.

6. Heat the broiler on high. Meanwhile, brush all surfaces of the cooked turkey with the remaining butter (melted). Broil the turkey for five minutes or until the skin is nicely browned and crisp. Once done, transfer onto a serving platter (warmed).

7. Serve drenched in cranberry sauce. Enjoy.

6 - Mouthwatering Sous Vide Beef for Dinner Recipes

Pesto and Asparagus Beef

Ingredients:

- Basil leaves, fresh (1 cup)
- Salt, kosher, divided (1 tablespoon)
- Lemon zest, freshly grated (1/2 tablespoon)
- Lemon juice, freshly squeezed (1/2 tablespoon)
- Olive oil, extra virgin (1/4 cup)
- Asparagus spears (20 pieces)
- Beef tenderloin, grass-fed, 6-oz. (4 pieces)
- Black pepper, freshly cracked (1/2 teaspoon)
- Garlic cloves, large, fresh, peeled (5 pieces)
- Parmesan cheese, grated (2 tablespoons)

Directions:

1. Fill the sous vide water oven before preheating to 134

degrees.

2. Meanwhile, sprinkle pepper and salt on the meat before placing inside cooking pouches (2 meat portions per pouch). Vacuum seal and then place in the sous vide water oven; allow the meat to cook for two hours.

3. Fill a pot with water and heat on high until boiling. Drop the basil leaves; after thirty seconds, remove and transfer immediately into an ice bath. Wring dry before chopping roughly and set aside in a blender. Do the same to the garlic.

4. In the blender, add the olive oil, salt (1 teaspoon), and Parmesan cheese. Process until well-combined and smooth before adding the lemon juice.

5. Meanwhile, fill a cooking pouch with the asparagus, making sure the asparagus pieces form a single layer. Add a little salt and 1/3 of the basil mixture. Vacuum seal and then drop into the sous vide water oven. Allow the asparagus to cook along with the meat for fifteen minutes. Once done, remove the steak and asparagus from the cooking pouches, and set aside on a

large plate.

6. Heat a grill pan on high before adding a little oil. Once heated through, add the steaks to sear on each side for about thirty to forty-five seconds. Transfer on a platter alongside the asparagus.
7. Serve topped with the remaining basil mixture (2/3 portion) and serve immediately.

Wagyu Fillets with Green Beans

Ingredients:

- Vegetable oil, high smoke point (1 tablespoon)
- Rosemary sprigs, fresh, divided (2 pieces)
- Beef tenderloin filets, Wagyu, 2-inches thick (2 pieces)
- Green beans, cooked (1 ½ cups)
- Butter, unsalted (2 tablespoons)
- Salt, kosher (1/4 teaspoon)
- Pepper, freshly cracked (1/4 teaspoon)

Directions:

1. Fill the sous vide water oven before preheating to 130 degrees. Meanwhile, fill a small cooking pouch with the cooked green beans.

2. Sprinkle pepper and salt on the fillets before placing them inside a cooking pouch (quart-size). After adding a rosemary sprig, vacuum seal the pouch and place in the sous vide water oven. Cook for two hours and thirty minutes to four hours.

3. Thirty minutes before the fillets' cooking time ends, add the pouch containing the green beans to the sous vide water oven.

4. Once done, take the fillets and green beans out of the sous vide water oven and transfer onto large plates. Use paper towels to pat dry the fillets. Set aside.

5. Heat a skillet on high before adding the vegetable oil. Once heated through, add the cooked fillets and sear for one minute on each side. Flip the fillets before adding in the butter as well as remaining rosemary sprig. Cook the fillets in the butter until basted and

crusted on all sides.

6. Serve the fillets alongside green beans and enjoy.

Western Style Burger

Ingredients:

Burger:

- Gorgonzola picante (1 ounce)
- Ground chuck, Angus (10 ounces)
- Frying oil, high smoke point (2 cups)
- Barbecue sauce (2 ounces)
- Butter (1 tablespoon)
- Pork roast (1/2 pound)
- Salt, kosher (1/4 teaspoon)
- Pepper, freshly cracked (1/4 teaspoon)
- Jalapeno peppers, fresh (2 pieces)
- Bread, focaccia (2 pieces)

6 - MOUTHWATERING SOUS VIDE BEEF FOR DINNER RECIPES

Onion rings:

- Paprika, Spanish (1/2 tablespoon)
- Cornstarch (1/2 cup)
- Pale ale (15 ounces)
- Cayenne pepper (1/2 teaspoon)
- Baking soda (2 teaspoons)
- Flour, all purpose, bleached (2 cups)
- Black pepper, freshly ground (1 teaspoon)
- Salt, kosher (2 ½ tablespoons)
- Baking powder (2 tablespoons)
- Yellow onion, large, peeled, sliced into quarter-inch slices (1 piece)

Directions:

1. Fill the sous vide water oven before preheating to 140 degrees.
2. Fill a small cooking pouch (quart size) with the pork.

Pour in the barbecue sauce before vacuum sealing the pouch. Drop in the sous vide water oven and allow the pork t cook for one to two days.

3. Sprinkle pepper and salt on the chuck burger, then mold into 2 patties. Place the patties inside a cooking pouch and freeze, unsealed, for two to three hours or until firm.
4. Meanwhile, decrease the water bath temperature to 130 degrees by adding ice cubes or iced water.
5. Take the patties out of the freezer. After vacuum sealing the pouch, place it in the sous vide water oven. Along with the pork, cook the patties for a minimum of one hour.
6. Heat a large skillet on medium-high before adding the oil (2 inches deep). In the meantime, sprinkle the onion slices with pepper and salt before dusting liberally with a small portion of the flour.
7. Place the rest of the flour in a large bowl. Add all the remaining ingredients to the batter. Stir continuously until well-combined and no lumps remain in the pan-

cake batter.

8. Once the oil temperature in the skillet reaches 350 degrees, add the onion slices (after being dipped into the prepared batter) and cook for about two to four minutes or until golden brown and crisp.

9. Remove the cooked onion slices. Add the fresh jalapeno and quickly toss in the oil. Once done (the skin is blistered), transfer onto a small dish.

10. As soon as the burgers are almost done, heat a broiler on high. Add the burgers and briefly cook until nicely seared and a bit charred on the surface.

11. Slice the focaccia into halves, then spread the cut sides with butter. Add to the broiler and sear, butter side down, alongside the burgers.

12. Place the unbuttered focaccia pieces on a platter. Brush a bit of barbecue sauce on the surface before topping with the patties and additional sauce, as well as pork and crumbled gorgonzola. Finish off each burger by adding an onion ring as well as a fried jalapeno and the buttered focaccia half.

13. Serve and enjoy.

Divine Smoked Beef

Ingredients:

- Beef brisket, trimmed (6 pounds)
- Meat rub (1/2 cup) – see below

Meat rub:

- Brown sugar (1 tablespoon)
- Salt, coarse (2 tablespoons)
- Onion powder (1 teaspoon)
- Paprika (3 tablespoons)
- Black pepper, freshly ground (1 tablespoon)
- Garlic powder (1 teaspoon)
- Cumin, ground (1 teaspoon)

Directions:

1. After filling the sous vide water oven with water, set

to 134 degrees to preheat.

2. Follow manufacturer's directions in setting up your device with hickory chips/ cakes/ pellets. For five minutes, use smoke produced by a smoking gun following food preparation.

3. Meanwhile, combine all ingredients for the meat rub in a medium bowl. Use this mixture to coat the brisket generously on all sides.

4. Place the seasoned brisket inside the cooking pouch. Vacuum seal before dropping the pouch inside the sous vide water oven. Allow the brisket to cook for forty-eight hours.

5. Once the brisket is done, remove the cooking pouch from the sous vide water oven and take out the brisket. Place in a closed container and smoke for thirty seconds. Allow the meat to soak up the smoke for five minutes.

6. Meanwhile, heat a skillet on high. Add the smoked brisket and cook for thirty to forty-five seconds or until the surface is crisp, seared, and caramelized.

7. After slicing, serve immediately and enjoy.

Smashing Ribs with Mashers

Ingredients:

Ribs:

- Salt, kosher (1/4 teaspoon)
- Pepper, freshly cracked (1/4 teaspoon)
- Celery stalk, trimmed, diced (1 piece)
- Tomato paste (2 tablespoons)
- Olive oil, extra virgin (1 tablespoon)
- Garlic cloves, peeled, minced (2 pieces)
- Red wine (4 ounces)
- Short ribs, 3-inches (4 pieces)
- Onion, peeled, diced (1/2 piece)
- Carrot, peeled, diced (1 piece)
- Thyme sprig (1 piece)

- Oil – to be used in searing

Mashers:

- Salt, kosher (1/4 teaspoon)
- Pepper, freshly cracked (1/4 teaspoon)
- Cream (2 ounces)
- Cheddar cheese (2 ounces)
- Red potatoes, creamer (1 pound)
- Butter (2 ounces)
- Chives, fresh, minced (1 tablespoon)

Directions:

1. Fill the sous vide water oven with water before setting to 185 degrees to preheat.
2. Rub pepper and salt on the short ribs, making sure all sides are seasoned well.
3. Heat a skillet (nonstick) on medium-high before adding the oil. Once heated through, add the

seasoned short ribs and cook until all sides are seared and browned. Once the ribs are done, transfer to a plate and cover to keep warm.

4. Wipe the pan before adding in olive oil (1 tablespoon). Stir in the vegetables and sauté until browned. Stir in the tomato paste as well and cook for one minute before pouring in the wine. Lower heat to medium and allow mixture to simmer until reduced. Transfer the mixture to a large bowl and place in the refrigerator for thirty minutes.

5. Pour the vegetable mixture into a cooking pouch. Add the ribs on top, making sure they form a single layer. Vacuum seal the pouch and place inside the sous vide water oven to cook for twelve hours.

6. Meanwhile, place the potatoes at the bottom of a cooking pouch. Sprinkle in the seasoning before vacuum sealing and dropping into the sous vide water oven. Allow the potatoes to cook for one hour before taking out of the water oven. Roughly press on the cooked potatoes (through the pouch) until mashed before slipping in the remaining ingredients. Mix well

and divide the potato mixture among 4 individual plates.

7. Take the cooked ribs out of the sous vide water oven. Place one rib on top of each masher-filled plate.

8. Meanwhile, pour the rib juices (from the pouch in which you cooked the ribs) into a pan. Heat on medium and cook until reduced. Drizzle the reduced liquid on top of the ribs.

9. Serve and enjoy.

7 - Scrumptious Sous Vide Pork for Dinner Recipes

Barbecue Pork Ribs

Ingredients:

- Olive oil, extra virgin – for cooking
- Ribs, country style, meaty (8 pieces)
- Barbecue sauce – see below
- Barbecue sauce:
- Salad oil (1 cup)
- Garlic, granulated (3 tablespoons)
- Pepper, white (2 tablespoons)
- Lemon juice (4 tablespoons)
- Salt, kosher (3 tablespoons)
- Ketchup (114 ounces)
- Cumin, ground (2 tablespoons)
- Oregano, dry (2 teaspoons)

7 - SCRUMPTIOUS SOUS VIDE PORK FOR DINNER RECIPES

- Molasses (1 cup)
- Black pepper, freshly ground (1 tablespoon)
- Onions, medium, peeled, minced (4 pieces)
- Brown sugar (2 ½ pounds)
- Cider vinegar (1 quart)
- Mustard, dry (4 tablespoons)
- Chile powder (1/3 cup)
- Cayenne pepper (1 tablespoon)
- Tabasco sauce (3 ounces)
- Honey (1 cup)
- Thyme, dry (1 tablespoon)

Meat rub:

- Sugar, granulated (2 tablespoons)
- Chile powder (2 tablespoons)
- Cayenne pepper (2 teaspoons)

- Cumin (2 tablespoons)
- Black pepper, freshly ground (1 tablespoon)
- Salt, kosher (1/4 cup)
- Paprika (2 tablespoons)
- Garlic powder (2 tablespoons)
- Mustard powder (1 tablespoon)

Directions:

1. Heat a soup pot (large) on medium before adding the salad oil. Once heated through, stir in the onions as well as brown sugar (1 tablespoon). Cook for five minutes or until the onions are caramelized.

2. Add the rest of the barbecue ingredients. Then stir well until the mixture is evenly combined. Turn heat down to low and allow the mixture to simmer for about an hour. Once done, pour the barbecue sauce into an airtight jar and place in the refrigerator.

3. Meanwhile, fill the sous vide water oven before preheating to 160 degrees.

4. Fill a small mixing bowl with the ingredients for the rib rub, Stir to combine and set aside.

5. Drizzle olive oil on the ribs before liberally brushing all sides with the prepared rib rub. Place the ribs inside large cooking pouches, making sure they form a single layer and then vacuum seal.

6. Drop the cooking pouches into the sous vide water oven. Allow the ribs to cook for eighteen to twenty-four hours.

7. Once the ribs are done, remove from the cooking pouches and set on a platter. Smother with the barbecue sauce and serve immediately.

Veggies and Pork with Blueberry Sauce and Sweet Potato Puree

Ingredients:

- Pork belly slab, 8-oz. (1 piece)
- Marinade:
- Cumin (1 teaspoon)

7 - SCRUMPTIOUS SOUS VIDE PORK FOR DINNER RECIPES

- Black pepper, freshly cracked (1 teaspoon)
- Fennel seeds (1 teaspoon)
- Cayenne pepper (1 tablespoon)
- Olive oil, extra virgin (1/4 cup)
- Salt, kosher (2 teaspoons)
- Cinnamon (1 tablespoon)
- Cloves, whole (3 pieces)
- Soy sauce, reduced sodium (1/2 cup)

Sweet potato puree:

- Butter, unsalted (2 tablespoons)
- Sweet potato, white, peeled, diced (1 piece)
- Cream (1/4 cup)
- Blueberry sauce:
- Sugar (1/4 cup)
- Vegetable stock (1/4 cup)

- Butter, unsalted (1 tablespoon)
- Blueberries, fresh/ frozen (1/2 cup)
- Soy sauce, low sodium (1 splash)
- Sesame chili oil (1/2 teaspoon)

Veggies:

- Mushrooms, wood ear (8 pieces)
- Mushrooms, nameko (4 ounces)
- Peppers, shishito (8 pieces)
- Vegetable stock (1 tablespoon)
- Butter, unsalted (1 tablespoon)

Directions:

1. Place the pork belly in a large bowl. Season with a mixture of pepper, cayenne, salt, cumin, and cinnamon. Add the fennel seeds, cloves, olive oil, and soy sauce, then toss until well-combined. Cover and place in the refrigerator to marinate overnight.

2. Fill the sous vide water oven before preheating to 155 degrees.

3. Remove the marinated pork belly from the refrigerator. Drain the marinade and then pat the meat with paper towels to dry. Transfer into a cooking pouch, vacuum seal, and drop into the sous vide water oven. Allow the pork belly to cook for four hours.

4. Meanwhile, heat a large pot on medium-high. Add salt (1 teaspoon) and bring water to a boil. Once boiling, add the potatoes; return to boiling and cook until tender.

5. Once the potatoes are done, strain and place in the food processor. Add salt, cream, and butter, then process until the potato mixture is well-combined. Return to the pot (after discarding the water) and heat on low to keep warm until served.

6. Heat a saucepot (1-quart) on medium-high before adding the sugar and blueberries. Once the sugar begins melting, gently mash the blueberries. Stir in the vegetable stock as well as sesame chili oil and soy sauce; cook for about two minutes or until heated

through.

7. Transfer the blueberry mixture into the food processor. Process until well-blended and then strain into the saucepot. Heat on medium and allow the blueberry mixture to cook until reduced to 1/2 and thickened. Once done, remove from heat and set aside.

8. Heat a saucepan on high before adding a little oil. Once heated through, stir in the shishito peppers as well as mushrooms. Cook for one minute before stirring in the vegetable stock (1 tablespoon). Allow the entire mixture to cook until reduced. Then stir in the butter (1 tablespoon). Once the butter has melted into the mixture, remove from heat and set aside.

9. Once the pork belly is done, remove from the sous vide water oven and cooking pouch, then transfer onto a plate. Set the pouch juices aside in a covered container.

10. Meanwhile, heat a frying pan on high before adding oil. Once the oil is heated through, add the pork belly and cook until the skin is seared. Gradually add the

reserved pouch juices and continue cooking until the pork belly is basted and its skin is crispy.

11. Serve and enjoy.

Brazilian Style Black Bean Stew

Ingredients:

- Onion, small, peeled, chopped (1 piece)
- Tomatoes, medium, trimmed, diced (3 pieces)
- Pork ribs, meaty, cooked, w/ meat pulled from bone (4 pieces)
- Sweet potato, medium, peeled, sliced (1 piece)
- Black beans, rinsed well (1 cup)
- Mango, peeled, seeded, cubed (1 piece)
- Bacon slices, thick, diced (4 pieces)
- Garlic clove, peeled, minced (1 piece)
- Red bell pepper, small, stemmed, seeded, diced (1 piece)

- Stock, vegetable/ stock (3 cups)
- Salt, kosher (1/4 teaspoon)
- Pepper, freshly cracked (1/4 teaspoon)
- Sausages, sweet, cooked, sliced (2 pieces)

Garnish:

- Arroz Braziliero, cooked (2 cups)
- Cilantro, fresh, chopped (a handful)
- Orange, fresh, sliced (1 piece)

Directions:

1. Fill the sous vide water oven before preheating to 195 degrees.
2. Meanwhile, heat a skillet on medium. Once hot, add the bacon and cook until browned and crisp.
3. Stir in the garlic and onions; cook for an additional two minutes or until fragrant and translucent. Turn off heat and allow the bacon mixture to slightly cool down.

4. Fill a large cooking pouch (1 gallon) with the bacon mixture as well as tomatoes, sweet potatoes, black beans, salt, pepper, red bell pepper, and vegetable stock. Vacuum seal before submerging into the preheated sous vide water oven and cook for three hours.

5. Meanwhile, fill another cooking pouch with the mangoes and cooked meats. Vacuum seal and drop into the sous vide water oven (after lowering its temperature to 158 degrees). Allow to warm along with the beans for half an hour.

6. Once done, transfer everything into a tureen (warmed). Stir to combine all cooked items. Serve topped with cilantro, orange, and Arroz Braziliero.

7. Enjoy.

Sage and Rosemary Pork Belly with Onions and Potatoes

Ingredients:

- Pork belly, rind on (1 pound)
- Olive oil, extra virgin (1 tablespoon)

- Sage, fresh, chopped roughly (1 teaspoon)
- Sea salt (1/4 teaspoon)
- Black pepper, freshly ground (1/4 teaspoon)
- Rosemary leaves, fresh (1 teaspoon)

Potatoes:

- White onion, medium, peeled, minced (1 piece)
- White wine, dry (1/2 cup)
- Sea salt (1/4 teaspoon)
- Pepper, freshly cracked (1/4 teaspoon)
- Olive oil, extra virgin (3 tablespoons)
- Potatoes, medium, peeled, chopped (3 pieces)
- Broth, beef, reduced sodium (2 cups)

Onions:

- Olive oil, extra virgin (4 tablespoons + 1 tablespoon)
- Water, filtered (2 ½ cups)

- Sea salt (1/4 teaspoon)
- Pepper, freshly cracked (1/4 teaspoon)
- Onions, cipollini, peeled (12 pieces)
- Vinegar, white wine (1/2 cup)
- Vinegar, balsamic (1 tablespoon)

Directions:

1. Heat a skillet on medium before adding the oil. Sauté for about five minutes or until a bit golden. Season with pepper and salt before pouring in the vinegar. Add the sugar as well. Then stir everything to combine. Allow the mixture to cook for five minutes or until all traces of vinegar are gone. Add water before covering and reducing heat to low. After five minutes, transfer the onions into a skillet greased with a little olive oil and heated on high. Add balsamic vinegar then cook until caramelized. Pour into a medium bowl and set aside.

2. Heat a medium gauge pot (heavy bottomed) on low before adding oil. Stir in the onion and cook for six to

eight minutes or until softened and fragrant. Stir in the potatoes and cook for another five minutes, making sure they are evenly coated. Pour in the white wine, stir, and allow to evaporate before pouring in the broth. Cook until the entire mixture is heated through and the potatoes are tender. Season with pepper and salt, then process into a puree with an immersion blender, food processor, or blender. Set aside in a large bowl.

3. Fill the sous vide water oven before preheating to 147 degrees.

4. Meanwhile, place the ingredients for the seasoning in a medium bowl. Stir to combine. Then rub the mixture all over the pork belly. Place the pork belly inside a cooking pouch, then vacuum seal and place in the preheated sous vide water oven to cook for eighteen to twenty-four hours.

5. Once the pork belly is done, take it out of the pouch and slice into 4 one-inch-thick portions. Set aside on a plate.

6. In the meantime, heat a heavy skillet (cast iron) on

high. Add olive oil and once heated through, add the pork belly with its rind side down. Cook until the rind is nicely seared, crunchy and golden.

7. Serve and enjoy.

Grilled Pork Ribs

Ingredients:

- Pork ribs, boneless (1 pound)
- Oregano, Mexican (1 tablespoon)
- Garlic cloves, peeled, chopped (2 pieces)
- Orange juice, freshly squeezed (1 cup)
- Onion, purple, peeled, sliced into rounds (1/2 piece)
- Achiote paste (2 ounces)
- Sazon seasoning, w/ salt, pepper & cumin (1 tablespoon)
- Vinegar, apple cider (1/2 cup)
- Olive oil, extra virgin (1/2 cup)

- Orange, sliced into rounds (1 piece)

Directions:

1. Fill the sous vide water oven before preheating to 149 degrees.

2. Pour the orange juice into a large bowl. Add the achiote paste, Sazon seasoning, and oregano, then whisk to combine into a smooth paste. Pour in the vinegar and whisk again to combine. Set aside.

3. Fill a large cooking pouch with the ribs. Pour in the prepared marinade as well as olive oil and garlic. Vacuum seal before submerging the pouch into the sous vide water oven. Allow the ribs to cook for twenty-four to forty-eight hours.

4. Heat a grill pan on high after generously oiling it. Once the ribs are tenderly done, transfer from the pouch and onto the grill pan to cook until both sides are seared.

5. Serve pork ribs with veggies on the side. Enjoy.

8 - Appetizing Sous Vide Lamb for Dinner Recipes

Lamb with Heirloom Tomatoes

Ingredients:

- Cherry tomatoes (1 pint)
- Salt, kosher, divided (1 tablespoon)
- Olive oil, extra virgin (1/4 cup)
- Rosemary sprigs, fresh (2 pieces)
- Chile flakes (1 teaspoon)
- Lamb rack, fresh (1 piece)
- Black pepper, freshly ground (1 teaspoon)
- Mint (1/2 bunch)
- Garlic cloves, peeled (2 pieces)

Directions:

1. Fill the sous vide water oven and then preheat to 136 degrees.

2. Meanwhile, sprinkle pepper and salt on the lamb, making sure all sides are evenly coated. Place inside a cooking pouch along with the rosemary sprigs, before vacuum sealing.

3. Drop the cooking pouch into the sous vide water oven. Allow the lamb to cook for two hours.

4. In the meantime, heat a pan on medium before adding olive oil. Add the garlic (thinly sliced), stir, and simmer for about three minutes. Once done, transfer into a cooking pouch along with the tomatoes, remaining salt, chile flakes, and mint. Vacuum seal and drop into the sous vide water oven as well to cook for one hour.

5. Once the lamb and tomato mixture are both done, remove from their pouches and transfer onto plates.

6. Heat a generously oiled grill pan on high before adding the lamb. Cook until all sides are seared, then transfer onto a platter. Set aside.

7. Meanwhile, drain the oil from the cooked tomatoes. After discarding the mint, place the tomatoes along-

side the lamb.

8. Serve and enjoy.

Lamb with Fig Syrup

Ingredients:

Lamb:

- Garlic cloves, peeled, minced (2 pieces)
- Cayenne, divided (1 teaspoon)
- Fennel pollen (2 tablespoons)
- Lamb racks, half ribs (2 pieces)
- Vegetable oil (1/4 cup)
- Rosemary, chopped finely (4 tablespoons)
- Black pepper, freshly ground (1 teaspoon)
- Salt, kosher, divided (2 ½ teaspoons)

Syrup:

- Fig preserves (1/2 cup)

- Vinegar, champagne (1/4 cup)
- Maple syrup, pure (1/4 cup)

Garnish:

- Walnuts, roasted, chopped finely (4 ounces)
- Goat cheese, young, crumbled (10 ounces)
- Parsley, Italian, chopped roughly (5 tablespoons)

Directions:

1. Fill the sous vide water oven before preheating to 134 degrees.
2. Place salt (2 teaspoons), garlic, pepper, cayenne (1/2 teaspoon), oil, fennel pollen, and rosemary in a medium bowl. Stir to combine.
3. Pat the lamb racks with paper towels to dry before rubbing the prepared spice mixture on all sides. Place inside a cooking pouch, then vacuum seal and submerge in the preheated sous vide water oven. Allow the lamb racks to cook for eighteen hours.
4. Meanwhile, fill a large saucepan (heavy bottomed)

with vinegar, salt (1/2 teaspoon), maple syrup, cayenne (1/2 teaspoon), and fig preserves. Stir to combine and then heat on medium. Allow the mixture to simmer before removing from heat and setting aside.

5. Once the lamb racks are done, remove from the sous vide water oven. Open the cooking pouch and slip the racks onto a large plate.

6. Heat a grill on high after generously greasing it with oil. Coat the lamb racks with fig syrup before cooking on the grill until nicely seared and browned.

7. Transfer the grilled lamb racks onto a platter. Coat again with fig syrup before slicing between the bones.

8. Transfer the ribs onto individual plates, making sure the ribs are evenly stacked. Top with chopped walnuts, crumbled goat cheese, and Italian parsley.

9. Serve and enjoy.

Pomegranate-Coffee Lamb

Ingredients:

- Brown sugar, packed (1/4 cup)
- Pepper, freshly cracked (1/4 teaspoon)
- Salt, kosher (1/4 teaspoon)
- Pomegranate juice (2 cups)
- Butter (1 tablespoon)
- Coffee, warm (1 cup)
- Balsamic vinegar (1/4 cup)
- Lamb racks, 1-oz. (2 pieces)
- Rosemary sprigs, fresh (2 pieces)

Directions:

- Place the brown sugar in a large bowl. Add the warm coffee and stir well. Once all the sugar granules are completely dissolved, add the pomegranate juice and balsamic vinegar. Stir again until well-combined, then reserve one cup of the mixture for using later (place in a small covered bowl and refrigerate).
- Place the 2 lamb racks in a large cooking pouch. Pour

in the remaining marinade and vacuum seal. Place in the refrigerator to marinate for four to twelve hours.

- Meanwhile, fill the sous vide water oven before preheating to 132 degrees.
- Drain the marinated lamb racks. Then pat dry with paper towels to remove any excess marinade. Season all sides of the racks with pepper and salt before placing into separate cooking pouches (gallon size). Include a fresh rosemary sprig in each cooking pouch before vacuum sealing, then drop into the sous vide water oven. Let the lamb racks cook for two hours.
- Meanwhile, take the reserved marinate out of the refrigerator. Pour into a skillet and heat on medium. Allow the marinade to boil before cooking for another five minutes or until reduced and thickened. Add the salt (1/8 teaspoon) and butter, whisk well until well-combined, and set aside.
- Set the broiler on high to preheat.
- Take the lamb pouches out if the sous vide water oven. Remove the racks from their pouches and

transfer to a large pan (broiler safe). Cook under the broiler for four to five minutes or until all sides are seared and browned.

- Place the broiled lamb racks in the skillet where you cooked the sauce. Turn the racks to make sure all sides are evenly coated. Then slice each rack into single chops.
- Serve right away with additional sauce on the side.
- Enjoy.

Salsa Verde Lamb Croquettes

Ingredients:

- Olive oil, extra virgin – as needed in cooking
- Thyme sprigs, fresh (4 pieces)
- Eggs, beaten slightly w/ 1 tbsp. of water (2 pieces)
- Pepper, freshly cracked (1/4 teaspoon)
- Breadcrumbs, panko (1 cup)
- Veal demi-glace (1/4 cup)

- Flour, all-purpose (1/4 cup) – for dusting before breading
- Lamb shanks (2 pieces)
- Salt, kosher (1/4 teaspoon)
- Salsa verde – see below

Salsa verde:

- Parsley, fresh, chopped coarsely (1 cup)
- Lemon zest, freshly grated (1 tablespoon)
- Salt, kosher (1/4 teaspoon)
- Basil, fresh, chopped (2 tablespoons)
- Olive oil, extra virgin (2/3 cup)
- Garlic cloves, medium, unpeeled (6 pieces)
- Anchovy fillets, blotted w/ paper towels to remove oil (4 pieces)
- Tarragon, fresh, chopped (1 tablespoon)
- Egg yolks (3 pieces)

- Pepper, freshly ground (1/4 teaspoon)

Directions:

1. Fill a small saucepan with cold water (1/2 inch deep). Add the garlic and cover the pan before heating on high. Once boiling, discard the water and add fresh water (1/2 inch deep). Allow to boil again before removing the garlic and rinsing under cold water. Once the garlic is cool enough to work with, remove its skin and chop into bits.

2. Place the chopped garlic in the food processor. Add the lemon zest, anchovies, tarragon, parsley, egg yolks, and basil. Process while you gradually stream in the oil. Once the mixture is just blended (it should not be smooth), add pepper and salt to season. Set aside.

3. Meanwhile, fill the sous vide water oven and preheat to 144 degrees.

4. Rub oil on the shanks before seasoning with pepper and salt. Place the seasoned shanks inside a cooking pouch (large). Add 2 sprigs of thyme into each pouch

before vacuum sealing. Place in the preheated sous vide water oven and allow to cook for forty-eight hours. Once done, drain the pouch juices into a covered bowl and set aside in the refrigerator. Transfer the shanks onto a platter, separate the meat from the bones, cover, and set aside.

5. Pour the reserved pouch juices in a saucepan and heat on medium. Stir and cook until reduced and thickened, then pour into a sauce pot. Stir in the glace and simmer on low. Once the sauce is thick enough that it sticks to a spoon, add in the lamb meat. Stir to combine, making sure the meat is evenly coated with the sauce.

6. Divide the meat into four equal portions. Place each lamb meat portion on a sheet of cling film. Then roll to form a tight cylindrical shape. Place all rolled lamb meats in the refrigerator to chill overnight.

7. Take the chilled lamb cylinders out of their wraps and set on a plate. Meanwhile, fill 3 separate bowls with panko crumbs, egg wash, and flour. Coat the lamb cylinders with the flour before dipping into egg wash.

Transfer into the bowl containing the panko crumbs and dredge, then place on a large plate.

8. Heat a deep fryer on high before adding the oil. Once the oil reaches 165 degrees, add the breaded lamb cylinders and cook until golden brown. Place on layers of paper towels to drain.
9. Serve lamb croquettes with the prepared salsa verde.
10. Enjoy.

Lamb with Cabbage and Potato Fondants

Ingredients:

Lamb:

- Salt, kosher (1/4 teaspoon)
- Pepper, freshly cracked (1/4 teaspoon)
- Lamb rump steaks, 8-oz. (4 pieces)
- Red currant jelly (2 tablespoons)

Cabbage:

8 - APPETIZING SOUS VIDE LAMB FOR DINNER RECIPES

- Leeks (2 pieces)
- Olive oil, extra virgin (3 tablespoons)
- Double cream (10 ounces)
- Mustard, whole grain (1 teaspoon)
- Cabbage head, Savoy (1 piece)
- Pancetta, smoked (7 ounces)
- Chicken stock, reduced sodium (8 ounces)
- Butter (2 tablespoons)

Potato fondants:

- Butter (10 tablespoons)
- Garlic cloves, peeled (3 pieces)
- Potatoes, Maris Piper (8 pieces)
- Chicken stock (14 ounces)
- Thyme sprig, fresh (1 piece)

Directions:

8 - APPETIZING SOUS VIDE LAMB FOR DINNER RECIPES

1. Fill the sous vide water oven before preheating to 135 degrees. Set the conventional oven to 395 degrees to preheat as well.

2. Peel the potatoes before slicing into equal-sized barrel/ cylindrical shapes. Place in a medium bowl.

3. Meanwhile, heat a roasting tray on high. Add the butter and allow to melt and foam before adding the potatoes. Cook for two to three minutes or until all sides are cooked through and golden brown.

4. Stir in the garlic as well as thyme. Pour in the chicken stock and mix well before transferring the roasting tray into the preheated conventional oven. Cook for about forty-five minutes or until the potatoes are tender, moist, and cooked through.

5. Sprinkle pepper and steaks on the rump steaks before placing inside cooking pouches. Vacuum seal and place in the preheated sous vide water oven and allow to cook for forty-five minutes to one hour.

6. Discard the cabbage's outer leaves and hard stalk before slicing into fine shreds. Set aside in a small bowl.

7. Meanwhile, heat a frying pan on medium. Add oil and allow to get extremely hot before adding the pancetta. Cook until nicely crisp and golden. Stir in the butter; once foaming, stir in the cabbage and leeks as well. Sprinkle pepper and salt and fry for about three to four more minutes or until the cabbage and leeks are softened and a bit golden.

8. Pour in the stock. Allow the mixture to cook for an additional five minutes or until the leeks and cabbage and cooked through and tender. Add the mustard and double cream, then cook for another five minutes or until the mixture is reduced to ¾ its original volume. Cover to keep warm.

9. Once the rump steaks are done, remove from the sous vide water oven and transfer onto a plate. Pat dry with paper towels and set aside.

10. In the meantime, heat a pan on high. Once extremely hot, add the rump steaks and cook until both sides are browned. Place on a platter and set aside.

11. Turn the heat of the same pan down to low before adding in the currant jelly. Allow to melt and then

brush on the rump steaks, making sure all sides are evenly coated. Cut the glazed rump steaks to form 8 slices.

12. Divide the cabbage among 4 plates. Top each with 2 rump steak slices and serve alongside the potato fondants.

13. Enjoy.

9 - Delicious Sous Vide Duck for Dinner Recipes

Duck Breast with Farro and Blackberry Jam

Ingredients:

Duck breast:

- Thyme leaves, fresh, picked (1/2 tablespoon)
- Black pepper, freshly ground (1/4 teaspoon)
- Red onions, julienned (1 cup)
- Salt, kosher (1/4 teaspoon)
- Garlic clove, peeled, smashed (1 piece)
- Parsley, chopped (1 tablespoon)
- Duck breasts, 8-oz. (2 pieces)
- Thyme sprigs, fresh, divided (4 pieces)
- Olive oil, extra virgin (1 tablespoon)
- Brown sugar (1 tablespoon)

9 - DELICIOUS SOUS VIDE DUCK FOR DINNER RECIPES

- Baby escarole heads, cut, washed (3 pieces)
- Shallots, minced (1 teaspoon)
- Farro, cooked (1 cup) – see below

Farro:

- Olive oil, extra virgin (1 tablespoon)
- Stock, chicken/ duck (2 cups)
- Carrot, peeled, diced finely (1/2 piece)
- Salt, kosher (1 teaspoon)
- Farro (3/4 cup)
- Celery stalk, trimmed, diced finely (1/2 piece)
- Turnip, peeled, diced finely (1/4 piece)

Blackberry jam:

- Sugar, granulated (3/4 cup)
- Blackberries, fresh (1 ¼ pounds)
- Lemon juice, freshly squeezed (1/2 tablespoon)

9 - DELICIOUS SOUS VIDE DUCK FOR DINNER RECIPES

Directions:

1. Place the berries in a colander and rinse under cool water. Transfer into a large bowl and toss gently with sugar. Over the bowl and place in the refrigerator; allow the berries to marinate overnight. Heat a large saucepan over medium. Then add the marinated berries to warm and soften. Remove the seeds with a food mill/ fine-mesh sieve before returning to the pan. Heat on medium, cook until thickened and keep warm.

2. Heat a saucepan on medium-high. Add the farro and cook until lightly toasted. Stir in the oil, carrot, celery, and turnip; cook for two minutes or until a bit tender. Pour in the water and add in salt. Stir to combine and allow the mixture to boil before reducing heat to medium-low. Cover and simmer for half an hour or until a small amount of liquid remains. Once done, fluff the farro with a fork and set aside.

3. Heat a saucepan on medium-high before adding the oil (1 tablespoon). Once heated through, stir in the onions. Arrange the onions into an even layer before

sprinkling the brown sugar on top. Stir and cook until the onions are tender and browned, then place in a covered bowl and refrigerate.

4. Fill the sous vide water oven and preheat to 132 degrees.

5. Sprinkle black pepper on the duck breasts before placing inside a cooking pouch. Add a thyme sprig on top of each duck breast. Vacuum seal the cooking pouch before submerging in the sous vide water oven. Allow the duck breasts to cook for thirty minutes to two hours. Once done, remove from the cooking pouch and transfer onto a plate; pat dry with paper towels, season with salt, and set aside. Meanwhile, pour the pouch juices into a small bowl and reserve.

6. Heat a large sauté pan on medium before adding the olive oil. Once heated through, stir in the garlic clove as well as the rest of the thyme sprigs. Once the oil starts smoking, turn heat down to low and add the duck breasts. Cook with their skin sides down for seven minutes. Once the fat is rendered, pour it off the pan. Flip the duck breasts on the other side to

cook for an additional minute. Once done, place on a platter, cover, and let sit.

7. Discard the fat from the pan and return to the stove. Heat on medium-high before adding the escarole. Cook until caramelized and a bit wilted. Then pour in the reserved pouch juices. Add the farro and caramelized onions as well as the shallots and garlic; stir and cook until the entire mixture is warmed through. Stir in thyme and parsley before covering to keep warm.
8. Drizzle the prepared blackberry sauce on the plate to form streaks. Place a small mound of farro and escarole mixture on one side, and top with the sliced duck breast. Add fresh thyme leaves and serve immediately.

Peking Style Duck Legs and Eggs

Ingredients:

Duck legs:

- Duck fat (8 tablespoons)
- Duck legs (8 pieces)

- Oil, high smoke point – for deep frying

Duck eggs:

- Duck eggs (6 pieces)

Cucumber spaghetti:

- Soya sauce, dark (2 teaspoons)
- Ginger, fresh, grated finely (1 teaspoon)
- Sesame oil (1 tablespoon)
- Cucumber (1 piece)
- Balsamic vinegar (2 teaspoons)
- Garlic clove, peeled, grated finely (1 piece)

Spring onion puree:

- Onions, Spanish, peeled, sliced finely (3 pieces)
- Spring onions, green, washed, sliced thinly (6 bunches)
- Pomace oil (2 tablespoons)

9 - DELICIOUS SOUS VIDE DUCK FOR DINNER RECIPES

- Double cream (10 ounces)
- Salt, kosher (1/4 teaspoon)

Dressing:

- Honey (1/4 cup)
- Soya sauce, dark (1/4 cup)
- Sesame oil (1 tablespoon)
- Ketchup (8 ounces)
- Orange juice, freshly squeezed (1/4 cup)
- Oyster sauce (1/4 cup)

Pancake crumb:

- Salt, kosher (1/4 teaspoon)
- Pastry sheets, feuille de brick, torn into bits (3 pieces)

Directions:

1. Fill the sous vide water oven before preheating to 180 degrees.

2. Fill 2 cooking pouches (large) with the duck legs (4 legs into 1 pouch). Pour in the duck fat before vacuum sealing the pouches, then place in the sous vide water oven. Allow the duck legs to cook for twelve hours.

3. Once the dusk legs are done, remove from the pouches and place on top of paper towels to drain off excess fat. Separate the meat (while still warm) from the bone and shred into thin strips before placing in a covered bowl. Set aside.

4. Turn the sous vide water oven temperature down to 147 degrees. Gently submerge the duck eggs to cook for one hour and ten minutes.

5. Meanwhile, heat a saucepan on medium before adding pomace oil; spread to form a thin film on the pan surface. Stir in the Spanish onions as well as salt (a pinch). Allow the onions to sweat for about four to five minutes or until translucent and softened.

6. Stir in the cream before turning the heat up to medium-high and allowing the mixture to boil. Stir in the spring onions; cook for about two to three minutes or until tender. Pour the mixture into the

blender and process until well-combined and smooth. Transfer the puree to a large bowl and place in the refrigerator.

7. After peeling and deseeding the cucumber, cut into long, extremely thin strands. Place in a large bowl and set aside.

8. Place all the ingredients for the cucumber strands in a small bowl. Stir to combine and set aside (toss with the cucumber later). Do the same with the ingredients for preparing the duck dressing.

9. Heat a deep fryer before adding the oil. Once the oil is heated to 356 degrees, add the shredded duck leg and cook until crispy. Once done, transfer onto a plate lined with paper towels and set aside.

10. Add pastry pieces to the same heated oil. Cook for half a minute, drain, and season with a bit of salt. Set aside.

11. Heat the pureed spring onion until warmed through, then divide among 4 plates. Gently toss the crispy duck meat with ½ of the dressing; divide among 4

portions and place each onto one plate (on top of the pureed spring onion).

12. Finish each plate by adding one duck egg, ¼ of the dressed cucumber strands, ¼ of the pancake crumbs, and ¼ of the remaining duck dressing.
13. Serve and enjoy.

Juniper Berry Duck

Ingredients:

- Thyme sprigs, fresh (3 pieces)
- Juniper berries, fresh-dried, red raisin (1/2 cup)
- Duck leg, quarter (1 piece)
- Salt, kosher (1/4 teaspoon)
- Spinach, fresh (1 cup)
- Orange zest, freshly grated (1 tablespoon)
- Orange fruit (1 piece)

Directions:

9 - DELICIOUS SOUS VIDE DUCK FOR DINNER RECIPES

1. Fill the sous vide water oven before preheating to 165 degrees.
2. Place the duck leg in a large bowl. Rub salt all over its sides before setting aside.
3. Use a vegetable peeler to strip off the zest from the orange. Section the fruit and place in a small bowl.
4. Place the juniper berries on a sheet of cling film. Top with the orange zest as well as thyme sprigs before loosely rolling. Place inside a small cooking pouch (quart size) and then top with a layer of orange sections. Add the salted duck leg in the middle before vacuum sealing the pouch.
5. Squeeze the orange pieces through the pouch before dropping the pouch into the sous vide water oven. Cook the duck leg for five to eight hours.
6. Once the duck leg is done, remove from the sous vide water oven. Drain the pouch juices into a skillet; set aside.
7. Meanwhile, set the broiler on high to preheat.

8. Unroll the juniper berry wrap and transfer the contents into the skillet containing the pouch juices. Heat on medium and cook the mixture until reduced. Season with pepper and salt, remove from heat and set aside.

9. Place the cooked duck leg below the preheated broiler to sear. Once done, transfer onto a platter.

10. Serve the broiled duck leg alongside a mound of fresh spinach. Smother with orange sauce and enjoy.

Easy Seared Duck

Ingredients:

- Shallots, chopped (2 tablespoons)
- Broccoli stalks, Chinese (2 pieces)
- Duck breasts, 8-oz. (4 pieces)
- Red wine (2 tablespoons)

Marinade:

- Cinnamon sticks (2 pieces)

9 - DELICIOUS SOUS VIDE DUCK FOR DINNER RECIPES

- Tong kwai herb (4 pieces)
- Sugar (1 teaspoon)
- Spring onions, green (2 pieces)
- Star anise pods (2 pieces)
- Ginger, fresh, minced (2 coins)
- Garlic cloves, peeled, mashed (4 pieces)
- Salt, kosher (1 teaspoon)

Ginger water:

- Water, filtered (3 ¼ ounces)
- Sugar (1/2 teaspoon)
- Ginger, sliced (3 ¼ ounces)
- Rice wine, Chinese (3 ¼ ounces)
- Salt, kosher (1/2 teaspoon)

Reduction base:

- Chicken, roasted (1/2 piece)

- Oyster sauce (2 teaspoons)
- Onion, large, peeled, sliced, sautéed (1/4 piece)
- Soy sauce, light (5 ounces)
- Chicken stock, reduced sodium (5 ounces)
- Apple, large, peeled, sliced, sautéed (1/4 piece)

Directions:

1. Place the duck breast inside a cooking pouch. Add the ingredients for the marinade before vacuum sealing and placing in the refrigerator to marinate overnight.
2. Fill the sous vide water oven and preheat to 133 degrees.
3. Add the duck breast pouch into the sous vide water oven and cook for fifty minutes.
4. Pour water into the blender. Add the ginger and process until well-combined into a paste. Pass the ginger paste through a sieve and set aside the liquid in a small bowl.
5. Fill a saucepan with the Chinese wine. Add the re-

served ginger liquid and stir to combine. Stir in the salt and sugar before heating the saucepan on medium-high. Allow the mixture to boil and then set aside.

6. Pour the ingredients for the reduction base into a pot. Stir to combine, heat on medium-high, and allow the mixture to simmer for an hour or until reduced to 2/3 its original volume. Pour into a sieve set atop a medium bowl; set aside.

7. Fill a pot with water and heat on medium-high. Once boiling, add the gai lan yo blanch for one minute. Remove and set aside in a small bowl.

8. Heat a skillet on medium-high before adding the shallots. Once fragrant, pour in the red wine as well as reduction base (100 milliliters). Stir and cook until the mixture is reduced to 2/3 its original amount. Remove from heat and set aside.

9. Meanwhile, heat a skillet on medium. Add the duck breast and cook until seared and browned on both sides. Once done, transfer to a plate.

10. Serve the duck leg alongside the blanched gai lan and topped with the reduction sauce.

Ginger Garlic Duck Breasts

Ingredients:

- Ginger garlic paste (4 teaspoons)
- Shallots, peeled (6 ounces)
- Coriander powder, ground (2 teaspoons)
- Coconut milk (3 ½ ounces)
- Salt, kosher (1/4 teaspoon)
- Coconut oil (1 teaspoon)
- Raisins (12 pieces)
- Tomato sauce (14 ½ ounces)
- Duck breasts (2 pieces)
- Turmeric (1 teaspoon)
- Curry leaves (2 stems)

- Cashew nuts, halved (2 pieces)
- Chili powder, Kashmiri (2 teaspoons)
- Garam masala (1/2 teaspoon)
- Onions, caramelized (1/2 cup)

Directions:

1. Trim the fat layers off the duck breasts before scoring the meats. Place in a large bowl and set aside.
2. Place ginger garlic paste (1 teaspoon) in a medium bowl. Add turmeric powder and salt, then stir well to combine. Pour the mixture onto the duck breasts, turning the latter to coat evenly on all sides. Cover and place in the refrigerator to marinate for thirty minutes.
3. Fill the sous vide water oven before preheating to 140 degrees.
4. Remove the marinated duck breasts from the refrigerator and transfer into a large cooking pouch. Vacuum seal before submerging in the preheated sous vide water oven. Allow the duck breasts to cook for

two hours and thirty minutes.

5. Meanwhile, heat a pan (heavy bottomed) on medium before adding the coconut oil. Once the oil is heated through, add the sliced shallots as well as curry leaves; sauté until golden brown.

6. Stir in the raisins, cashew nut, and the rest of the ground spices and ginger garlic paste. Cook for an additional minute before adding in the duck breast. Cook until the surfaces are nicely seared.

7. Pour in the tomato sauce as well as a small amount of water. Stir and allow the mixture to simmer until thickened, before stirring in the salt and coconut milk.

8. Serve the duck meat over a pool of ginger garlic sauce. Top with caramelized onions and enjoy.

10 - Conclusion

Now you know everything there is to know about cooking your food the sous vide way, so any misgivings you may have about giving it a go should be tossed out the kitchen window.

Not sure about the safety of cooking bags or pouches used to hold your ingredients? Rest assured that sous vide plastic containers are made of inert polyethylene material, which means that it does not contain harmful substances like phthalate or BPA that can leach into your "sous videlicious" fares.

You do have to be extra careful with refrigerating your sous vide cooked food. Once you open the pouch, make sure to consume the contents right away or within three days. Sticking your sous vide cooked food in the refrigerator for more than that time frame only gives bacteria the opportunity to flourish and cause you potential harm.

Don't get yourself tied up in choosing the most digitally enhanced sous vide immersion circulator or water oven. The point of cooking with the sous vide method is to be able to cook your food perfectly each and every time after setting your cooking device to your target time and temperature.

10 - CONCLUSION

Your immersion circulator or water oven can be left alone to work on your food and give you the exact results you want, even if you don't adjust the controls.

Lastly, give yourself a chance to breathe and relax in the knowledge that it is perfectly fine if it takes you several tries before achieving perfection. Once you master the sous vide method of cooking your favorite dishes, eating gourmet quality food at home every day and night of your life is possible.

Thank You

As we reach the end of this book, I want to say thanks for reading this book.

I want to get this information out to as many people as possible. If you found this book helpful, I would greatly appreciate you leaving me a review. This helps others find the book as well.

Disclaimer

This document is geared towards providing exact and reliable information in regards to the topic and issue covered. The publication is sold on the idea that the publisher is not required to render an accounting, officially permitted, or otherwise, qualified services. If advice is necessary, legal, financial, medical or professional, a practiced individual in the profession should be ordered.

This information is not presented by a financial or medical practitioner and is for entertainment, educational and informational purposes only. The content is not intended as a substitute for professional medical advice, diagnosis, or treatment. Always seek the advice of your physician or other qualified health care provider with any questions you may have regarding a medical condition. Never disregard professional medical advice or delay in seeking it because of something you have read.

The information provided herein is stated to be truthful and consistent, in that any liability, in terms of inattention or otherwise, by any usage or abuse of any policies, processes, or directions contained within is the solitary and utter responsibility of the recipient reader. Under no circumstances will any legal responsibility or blame be held against the publisher for any reparation, damages, or monetary loss due to the information herein, either directly or indirectly.

Last Updated: 24.Nov.2017

www.ingramcontent.com/pod-product-compliance
Ingram Content Group UK Ltd.
Pitfield, Milton Keynes, MK11 3LW, UK
UKHW021920190726
13853UKWH00002B/767